Legal In<sup> (barcode: MW00389557)

Table of Contents

Introduction

In 2009, we took an escorted tour to Tallinn, Estonia; Helsinki, Finland; and St. Petersburg, Russia. We were amazed at the beauty of St. Petersburg, and we were sorry the tour didn't also include Moscow. Well one day last year, we received a brochure in the mail from Viking River Cruises outlining a 13-day river cruise that started in St. Petersburg and ended in Moscow. We thought: what a great way to not only revisit a wonderful city, but to tour other parts of Russia we hadn't yet had the chance to explore. Jon especially liked the idea of visiting the Cosmonaut Museum in Moscow, though he's always been interested in Russia in general. We had never done any type of river or ocean cruising and we thought this would also be a good way to try it. So we took the cruise in August 2016, and that is how this book came to be written.

We love to travel and it is our pleasure to try to impart that love of traveling to you through our books. They are not meant to be guidebooks that tell you what sites to see and what hotels to choose. Rather, they're meant to supplement the information you'll find in guidebooks and hopefully encourage you to visit the countries we've visited. This book is slightly different from our others in that it doesn't provide a lot of tips to things we had to discover on our own. Instead it describes sites we saw in a country that tends not to be chosen by too many Americans as the first place they want to visit. And it gives our impressions of a river cruise in that country in case you're considering that mode of transportation for your own trip.

Jon and I decided to share our experiences of our recent trip to Russia so that you might get some ideas for your future travels. If you've been considering going to Russia, this may help you decide if it's a place you'd like to go. If you've been considering a river cruise, this may help you decide if a river cruise is for you. We comment on both the positive and negative.

Note: We have no relationship with Viking River Cruises, other than having gone on this cruise. Any comments we make about it, the staff or the cruise itself are strictly our opinion based on our experiences. Our purpose in doing so is not to promote the company, but to give an account of our vacation and what we experienced.

So you know who's writing this book, I'll tell you that we're a middle-aged couple around Medicare age, but we're in denial all the way. As my doctor likes to say, we're "active seniors." We've been around long enough to have done a fair amount of national and international traveling, but not so old that we can't have amazing adventures. We've traveled independently and on escorted tours. Although the cruise was experienced by both Jon and Marcy, and this book was written by both, it will be narrated with one voice, that of Marcy.

Arrival

We were met at the St. Petersburg airport by a Viking representative. When everyone from our flight who was on the cruise arrived, we boarded an air-conditioned bus for a 30-minutes ride to the ship. The representative gave everyone a small water bottle for the ride – a nice touch.

It was somewhat disappointing to find out that the ship was not docked close to downtown St. Petersburg. There were some closer docks that had been used in earlier years, but they weren't able to accommodate a ship of the *Truvor's* size. So we were "out in the suburbs" somewhat. Check-in on the ship was very quick, and thankfully our room was ready when we arrived, since we had left Chicago over 12 hours earlier.

The Ship

When we made our trip reservations we chose a room with a veranda, assuming that would be a nice place to sit outside and watch the scenery as we sailed by. We found the next morning upon opening our curtains that another Viking ship had docked while we were sleeping. So our view now consisted of someone else's veranda. And occasionally our view would consist of another person sitting on their veranda reading! We also discovered that occasionally we had to walk through that ship's lobby to get from our ship to land. At one point there were three Viking ships docked side by side and we had to walk through the lobbies of the other two to reach land.

Our room had a queen-size bed with a small end table on each side and a bright reading light overhead. On the wall opposite the bed was a console containing shelves and a mini-fridge. On top of the console were the handsets and earphones to be used with shore excursions (so the guides didn't have to shout), two water bottles that were replenished by the housekeeping staff whenever they were empty, and plenty of space to put a camera, backpack or whatever. There was also a large wall-mounted flat-screen TV. A hairdryer was located in a drawer. The room had lots of electrical outlets for charging electronic items. There was a column in the middle of the room that we had to walk around. In truth, it became less noticeable as time wore on, but it did have a small platform at the bottom that Jon tripped over at least once. There was lots of shelf space for our clothes, but I was glad we had the foresight to bring a few plastic hangers from home because there weren't enough in the closet.

Since I'm someone who can't stand being hot, I loved the fact that our room had an amazing air conditioner. As a matter of fact, we had to turn it down to keep from freezing!

The bathroom was quite small with a tiny shower, but the showerhead was hand-held and swiveled so you could keep the water from flooding the bathroom. There was also a retractable clothes line in the shower. The bathroom had a magnifying mirror which some women would view as a nice addition; however, it didn't light up so I found it basically useless. In terms of towels, there were one wash cloth, one hand towel and one bath towel per person. If you're one who likes an additional towel to wrap your washed hair, you'll need to bring a quick-dry towel from home. The bathroom came equipped with a shower cap, shampoo, conditioner, body lotion, a small bar of soap and shower gel. There was a wall cabinet for storage, as well as a shelf underneath the sink. There was space underneath the bed to store our suitcases so they were out of the way during the cruise but accessible if needed.

The room and bathroom were kept immaculately clean during our voyage. The cleaning staff came in during the day while we were out and again in the evening to straighten up, provide new towels if wanted, and give us turn-down service. I joked to Jon that they didn't provide chocolates on our pillows. Well, on the fourth night they did, with a welcome note. I'm not sure why they waited so long to leave the note; perhaps it was because that was the night we left St. Petersburg. And unfortunately we only got the chocolate on that one night. The staff also kept on top of replacing used up amenities, which was nice.

There were two restaurants for breakfast. The main restaurant, the Neva Restaurant, had a full breakfast buffet, with a variety of juices, hot and cold cereal, pastries and breads, made-to-order omelets, etc. There were also options we could order off the menu. The Panorama Bar had a continental breakfast of juice and pastries. The only cereal available was something that looked like oatmeal, but was cold and to me tasted like tuna fish. These same two venues were available for lunch, the Neva having a more extensive selection and the Panorama Bar being available as a lighter/quicker option. I have to say, even the dessert in the Panorama Bar was a lighter option. To us, it looked more like a sample size than a full size dessert. But of course, no one would've stopped us from going back and getting another one from the buffet.

Dinner was only available in the Neva Restaurant and consisted of a variety of menu choices. Three entrée choices were always available, and three additional entrée selections changed daily. Just outside the Neva Restaurant was a coffee/tea station with pastries in the morning and cookies in the afternoon. The cookies were a good addition when the sample size dessert from the Panorama Bar wasn't enough (or let's face it – even if it was).

The ship had a gift shop but don't expect to be able to purchase any toiletry items you may have forgotten to pack. It's a gift shop in the strictest sense of the word, with nice souvenir items you may want to bring home for yourself or others. It was stocked with matryoshka (nesting) dolls, lacquer boxes, amber jewelry, etc. The shop also had some nice items for the ship guests to purchase including a brief guidebook to the sites we'd visit as well as a useful map of the entire trip. For those looking for something to read, there was also a small library onboard with a selection of books in English mostly concerning Russian culture, flora and fauna, and history. Seating areas with small tables and four chairs were located at both ends of the ship, and there were two computers available for passengers' use with free Internet service. Viking called this an Internet Café. I call it a computer desk. There were four levels on the ship, and an elevator was available for those who didn't want to take the stairs.

Regarding those items you may have forgotten to pack: Well, I couldn't find the second tube of toothpaste I packed so I asked for one at the reception desk. They did provide me with a very tiny one (and a toothbrush) that lasted for three days.

There was an outdoor area on the top deck furnished with tables and chairs. Blankets were available on some of the chairs so passengers could sit out there in chilly weather (which was in abundance in St. Petersburg). There was also a lounge which was used for evening cocktails as well as for lectures about Russia given by the staff. During the cocktail hours, passengers were entertained by a singer and piano player.

The ship staff offered water bottles every day as we were leaving for our shore excursions, and there was a rack of large umbrellas for those who neglected to bring one from home. For shore excursions, the passengers were divided into six groups. Each group was assigned a bus and tour escort who accompanied them on each excursion. This was our assigned bus for the entire trip. We also had local guides with us for each tour.

For those of you who want to know such things, we learned one night during a Q&A with the ship's captain that the *Viking Truvor* was built in 1987 in East Germany. It has three 1,000 horse power diesel engines and makes five to seven kilometers an hour when going upstream. The ship has a crew of over 100 who sleep below deck and stay on the ship for six months.

Viking Truvor

Day 1 – August 10 – St. Petersburg

We had a 6:00 p.m. orientation with the onboard Viking staff. There were about 200 people on our cruise, most seeming to be our age or older. They informed us that we would be going through 17 locks on the waterways between St. Petersburg and Moscow. They also explained about the use of the handsets and earphones we found in our rooms. We were told to bring them on each shore excursion to listen to the local guides. This proved to be much easier and more civilized than trying to hear a guide shouting to a crowd of people.

We then had dinner in the ship's dining room. Given the time change between Chicago and St. Petersburg, we were ready for bed after the meal. Throughout the trip the restaurant's wait staff proved to be unfailingly polite, efficient and very helpful. Interestingly they came from many countries (including the Philippines). And it's a very long working season since they don't leave the boat for six months.

Day 2 – August 11 – St. Petersburg

Before we could begin having fun, we had to deal with some serious business - the safety drill. We were instructed to put on the life vests from our rooms and stand by our doors. Ship staff came by and showed us the correct way to tie them. Jon and I had no problem, but we noticed a couple of the older guests who did.

Finally we were able to begin our shore excursion which this day consisted of a trip to the State Hermitage Museum, one of the largest art museums in the world. The Hermitage is housed in the former Winter Palace of the tsars on the Palace Square. The location of our ship's dock was not near St. Petersburg's city center which meant that each venture into the city was about an hour long. There was much more traffic in St. Petersburg than we expected, but maybe we should have, given that it is a city of over five million people. We did get a pretty good view of the famous cruiser Aurora (built in 1900) and the Peter and Paul Fortress (built in 1703 by Peter the Great) on the way in.

Once we got there, we disembarked from our bus in the rain (which seems to be a constant in St. Petersburg along with 60 degree temperatures). We had to wait in line about 10 minutes until our reserved admitting time. This is important to note because our guide didn't tell us about the waiting time outside, and some people chose to leave their jackets and umbrellas on the bus rather than go through the hassle of checking them in the museum (which is mandatory). As a result, they got a little cold and wet while waiting in line. The temperature in the museum is quite warm, so if you dress for the cool weather outside, you may be too warm inside.

Once inside, we were greeted by a wall of humanity. The crowds were massive! One wonders what true art lovers must think of these hordes of people rushing around them when trying to look at some truly famous works of art. We noticed a large number of tourists from China, so many in fact that our tour escort said he'd soon have to learn Chinese.

Our time in the Hermitage consisted of a 1-1/2 hour guided tour and one hour of free time, which of course didn't come close to covering the museum; but we saw a few of the highlights such as Michelangelo's Crouching Boy sculpture and Rembrandt's The Sacrifice of Isaac painting. Of special interest is the famous 18th century Peacock Clock. Although it still works, it is only wound on special occasions. As we saw in a video next to the exhibit, a peacock, a rooster and an owl sit on a tree and move in impressive fashion on the hour.

Peacock Clock

That evening after dinner onboard in the Neva Restaurant, we boarded our buses again for a return trip to the Hermitage, this time to see a performance of Swan Lake at the Hermitage Theatre. This is an intimate theater built in the 18th century for Catherine the Great. The best part of this ballet was the performance of the ballerina dancing the parts of Odette/Odile. She normally dances with the Mariinsky Ballet (known under Soviet times as the Kirov Ballet), and she was outstanding. The rest of the dancers were average. But still it was a thrill being there and seeing such a well-known Russian ballet in St. Petersburg.

Upon returning to the ship about 11:00, we found that desserts had been set up for everyone in the Neva Restaurant. After two weeks of cruising, we discovered to our dismay that this was a one-time deal.

As an interesting aside, someone asked one of our guides if he was born in St. Petersburg. He said no, he was born in Leningrad. He then showed us his passport, which still lists Leningrad as his birthplace.

Day 3 – August 12 – St. Petersburg

On this sunny but cold (50ish degrees) day, we took a bus to Catherine's Palace in suburban Pushkin, a short ride from our ship. This Catherine is not Catherine the Great, but Catherine I, Peter the Great's wife. He built it for her in 1717. In the 1750s, it was greatly expanded by their daughter Empress Elizabeth who used it as her principal summer residence. It's now used by Vladimir Putin for entertaining guests both foreign and domestic. We toured the interior of the palace, after putting on shoe coverings. Afterwards we had time to walk through the beautiful gardens surrounding the palace.

Catherine's Palace in Pushkin

The palace was destroyed by the Nazis during World War II, and there are photographs inside the palace showing the destruction. Its ornate décor has been meticulously restored, including the famous Amber Room, a room decorated with genuine amber panels, which is considered a highlight of the palace. The original panels were stolen by the Germans during World War II and subsequently lost. The Amber Room was rebuilt in 2003 for $12 million. Photographs are allowed throughout the palace with the exception of the Amber Room. According to our local tour guide, although some parts of the Amber Room were discovered after the war, any pieces now found must be purchased from the post-war owner.

Another highlight of Catherine's Palace is the Great Hall or Hall of Light, a room that takes up the entire width of the palace. It has gilded stucco on the walls, and alternating windows and mirrors. A number of wall sconces help provide a lot of light. The ceiling is covered with a fresco called The Triumph of Russia. The hall was used for important dinners and balls.

Great Hall at Catherine's Palace

After returning to St. Petersburg and having lunch on board the ship, we went on a walking tour of the city. Given a choice between a bus tour and a more intensive walking tour, we chose the latter. The bus tour was selected by those passengers who didn't have the ability, or the inclination, to walk long distances. The walking tour lasted five hours. After riding the bus to the metro and taking the metro to the city center, the tour was all walking. The metro was an adventure in itself. Twenty-plus of us crammed into a couple of metro cars at that stop. And though we'd been warned that the trains took off very quickly and we should hang on to something, Jon didn't right away and bounced off a drunk guy who was sitting there shuffling cards. Fortunately the guy was soon snoring and didn't bother us at all, though some of the other passengers looked askance at him. The metro cars are very old school, but they also accelerate very quickly. Hang on.

Once we got off the train in the city center, we walked to Nevsky Prospekt, the main shopping street, where we visited an amazing food hall and coffee house called Kupetz Eliseevs. The center of the room consists of tables and red chairs for dining around a giant pineapple tree. Around the perimeter are arrangements of teas, caviars, wines, pastries and chocolates. My favorite was the chocolate shoes.

Chocolate Shoes in Display Case at Kupetz Eliseevs

After spending too short a period of time in the food hall, we walked down a short pedestrian-only street with several sidewalk cafes. We can't imagine that sidewalk cafes are very successful in St. Petersburg with its cool climate and frequent rain. (This is probably a good time to mention to you that you need to pack for all kinds of weather in St. Petersburg. This particular afternoon started out sunny with the temperature in the high 60s. Then out of the blue a downpour occurred, and the temperature dropped. It's a good idea to carry an umbrella or rain jacket with you, even if the chance of rain is only 20%. One of our tour escorts described St. Petersburg weather as nine months of expectation and three months of disappointment.) Something we didn't expect to see in St. Petersburg was a Harley rally which was taking place across the street from Kupetz Eliseevs. Labeled "St. Petersburg Harley Days" on a large banner, the festival seemed to be attracting a big crowd. I guess Harleys are popular everywhere.

Now back to our walk. After the pedestrian-only street, we turned the corner and came upon a tsarist-era building that currently houses the Museum of Hygiene. This museum was established in 1919 to show people the value of good personal hygiene and health. If you're interested in unusual museums, St. Petersburg has a number of them. Besides this one, there are the Museum of Vodka which conveys the history of vodka-making since the 12th century; the Metro Museum which gives the history of the city's metro system; and the Museum of Bread which presents the history of bread making. Unfortunately we didn't have time to visit any of them.

Another highlight of our walking tour was the Church of our Savior on the Spilled Blood. This church which has distinctive blue, white, gold and green domes was built on the spot where Tsar Alexander II was assassinated in 1881. There was a lot going on at the church, which makes sense since it's such a popular spot. In addition to the crowd of tourists, there were two musicians playing. There was also a private wedding taking place in the park behind the church.

Domes of the Church of Our Savior on the Spilled Blood

We took a short break here, which allowed us to look over the many vendors along the canal outside the church. There was no shortage of matryoshka (nesting) dolls for sale, but we learned later from one of the ship's escorts that there are definite differences in the quality of those dolls. There were also many souvenirs with Putin on them – mugs with his mug on them, tee-shirts with him riding a grizzly bear and toting a gun on his back, playing cards and refrigerator magnets. According to our ship escorts, Russians have a positive attitude toward Putin, telling us that the economy had improved for the average person under him. (See the appendix at the end of the book.) For a brief minute, we thought about buying the tee-shirt with the bear-riding Putin on it and sending it to Donald Trump signed, "All my love, Vlad." But then our common sense took hold and we relegated that idea to the list of things we'd like to do that are better left undone.

Putin Souvenir Mugs

Continuing our walk, we arrived at a bridge along the Moyka River in an area that looked familiar to us. We were thrilled to discover our internal compasses were still working after seven years away from the city, having arrived at the area where we had stayed on our first trip there. We walked by the house at number 12, which is where the poet Alexander Pushkin lived for a couple years and where he died after being wounded in a duel. And just past this building is the Pushka Inn, our hotel on our first visit. Right around the corner from these buildings is the immense, beautiful Palace Square, site of historical events such as Bloody Sunday in 1905 and the October Revolution in 1917. The Palace Square is currently used as a site for concerts and parades, but it is as impressive as ever.

As previously mentioned, the Palace Square is the location of the Winter Palace which now houses the State Hermitage Museum. Across from the Winter Palace is another building which used to house the Imperial Army Government Staff and now houses government offices. There is an archway in the Government Staff building called the Triumphal Arch. You can walk through it to get to Nevsky Prospekt. In the middle of the square is the Alexander Column, a monument to Russia's victory over Napoleon. At this point in our tour it was raining pretty hard so we didn't linger in the square.

Government Staff Building with Triumphal Arch

After leaving the square we came upon a couple of interesting statues. One is located on the Admiralty Embankment of the Neva River and was donated by the Netherlands to replace one destroyed by the Bolsheviks in 1918. It's a statue of Peter the Great as a boat builder and was designed to celebrate his role in Russia's shipbuilding industry. The other is called The Bronze Horseman and is the most famous one of Peter the Great. Located in Senate Square, this statue was commissioned by Catherine the Great. It took 12 years to complete.

The Bronze Horseman

Our walk ended at St. Isaac's Church, the largest Russian Orthodox cathedral in St. Petersburg. It took 40 years to build and was completed in 1858. If you're walking around St. Petersburg and see a golden dome in the distance, you're looking at St. Isaac's Church. The church currently houses a museum and only holds services on religious holidays.

Actually our walk didn't quite end at the church. It ended at the pit stop after the church. It costs to use many of the public toilets in Russia, but it's not expensive. This one cost 20 rubles – about 31 cents. One of our fellow passengers who entered with Jon asked the attendant if she accepted American dollars. She just pointed at the sign that said in English, "20 rubles". So it's best to have some with you before starting your first shore excursion. There's no ATM on the ship, but there was one at a souvenir store just a few steps from where the ship was docked. Or you can get them at an ATM at the airport.

Day 4 – August 13 – St. Petersburg

This partly sunny and cool day was spent at Peter the Great's palace Peterhof, about a 50-minute drive from our ship. You'll see a line of vendors on the way in. To give you an idea of its grandeur, Peter's inspiration for his palace was the French palace of Versailles. Peter the Great built the palace, but it was expanded by his daughter Empress Elizabeth (yes the same Elizabeth who expanded Catherine's Palace. I guess she really liked glitz and glamour.) As with Catherine's Palace, Peterhof was destroyed during World War II by the Germans. Many of the fountains were destroyed and the Grand Palace was burned. There are photos here depicting how it looked after the war before it was restored.

Among Peterhof's attractions is the Grand Palace. It has many ornate rooms which we toured, but our favorite was Peter's wood-paneled study, which looked very welcoming and intimate. Once again, we had to wear shoe coverings before touring the rooms.

The grounds have spectacular gardens, walking paths and fountains. At 11:00 a.m., all the fountains are turned on simultaneously as the St. Petersburg Anthem is played. All the fountains are run by gravity from a spring behind the Grand Palace. Of course this attracts a multitude of tourists, who cluster around the fountains waiting for them to go off.

Another site at Peterhof is Monplaisir, Peter's original palace and his favorite living quarters. It's located below the Grand Palace on the Gulf of Finland, a short walk from the Grand Palace through a lovely garden. Peter preferred Monplaisir because he could view his naval vessels from there.

Grand Palace and Fountains at Peterhof

After walking around the grounds for a bit, I decided to buy some ice cream from a vendor in the park. The vendor gave me two bags of chestnuts with the ice cream bar I selected, and we have yet to figure out why. When I ordered the bar, he asked what to me sounded like nutty or smooth. Not wanting nuts in my ice cream, I answered smooth. Then he gave me the bar and the two bags of chestnuts. Obviously there was a language barrier.

After having lunch later on the ship, Jon and I decided to go for a walk. The ship wasn't docked in a particularly good spot for walking and there was nothing scenic to see; but we felt we needed to do something. So we walked on a path between the water and the road with cars whizzing quickly by. The dock is near an old industrial area, with abandoned factories along the road and some barges unloading coal along the river. There were also a few bikers along this path who ventured down to the river in order to fish, but we didn't see them catch anything.

After four days docked in St. Petersburg, the ship finally got underway for our next stop at about 6:00 in the evening. Though we enjoyed St. Petersburg a lot, it was great to finally be moving. This portion of the trip took us from the Neva River in St. Petersburg to Mandrogy on the Svir River, where we would arrive about noon the next day. Mandrogy lies between Lake Ladoga and Lake Onega, the two largest lakes in Europe. The view on our way to Mandrogy consisted of nautical and lumber industry buildings and small towns, which eventually gave way to dense forest.

We were told we would be passing a castle near Shlisselburg that used to be political prison at about 10:15 that night. We thought it would be lit up but it wasn't. If another passenger hadn't noticed it, I probably would have missed it completely in the dark.

There was a welcome cocktail party at 6:15 before that day's 6:30 orientation in the bar. We opted to skip cocktails and arrive at 6:30. It turns out we shouldn't have skipped it because the cocktail party included a presentation, which the Viking staff neglected to mention. When we got there, they were introducing the ship's staff (ship's captain, chef, and our tour escorts.). We may not have missed anything really important, but it would have been nice to know it was more than just a "cocktail party".

Our sleep that night was interrupted by the ship rocking and rolling. There were unusually high swells and rain on Lake Ladoga, making for an interesting night of sleeping – or lack thereof.

Day 5 – August 14 – Mandrogy

Before our arrival in Mandrogy, we spent a couple hours listening to presentations by two of our escorts. These took place throughout the journey and were excellent. The first was on Russia and its geography, climate and politics. The second concerned Russian food and souvenirs (yes!). We learned how to tell cheap matryoshka dolls from good ones (the more intricate the hand painting the better). We were told that lacquer boxes, which our escort referred to as "the legacy of Russia," are made of papier mache, lacquered and hand painted and come from four regions, each with its own style. The best ones are hand painted and signed by the artist. Cheap versions have scenes that are glued on and lacquered over rather than hand painted. We also learned that vodka, boxes made out of birch wood, and Faberge-style eggs make good souvenir gifts.

Mandrogy, where we arrived about noon, is a reconstructed village which exists primarily for tourists on river cruises to get a sense of life in a typical Russian village. The original village was destroyed by the Nazis in World War II and rebuilt in 1996 by a Russian businessman as a traditional Russian village. Some of the ship's passengers took advantage of an optional tour to Mandrogy's banya or bath house. In a hot steam room, your body will be brushed with a special broom made of leaves dipped in cold water, in order to improve your circulation. After you leave the banya, cold water is poured over you. Then you can run into the frigid water of the Svir River. Sounds like fun, doesn't it? Well, some people thought it was, but we decided to walk around the village instead.

On our walk we saw that Mandrogy has some colorful houses, a hotel, a restaurant, a vodka museum (with over 2,500 brands of vodka), a bread museum, a windmill and a number of people busy at work making Russian crafts. We found beautiful matryoshka dolls and hand-painted eggs. Our favorite shop was the Craftman's Workshop where they were creating beautiful items for sale. The most incredible were a series of nesting eggs featuring scenes from

19th century Russian naval battles. Though the painter was willing to negotiate on the price, they were still out of our price range. And spoiler alert to our relatives – we bought some Christmas presents.

Mandrogy is also home to the world's largest felt boot. It's 10-1/2 feet high and about seven feet long. It's a Russian traditional winter boot made of the wool that is used to make such boots in Russia. It's just bigger. We have no idea why it's there.

Marcy In Front of the World's Largest Felt Boot

We left Mandrogy about 5:00 in the evening, continuing our cruise along the Svir River to Lake Onega, the second largest lake in Europe. In the center of that lake lies Kizhi Island where we arrived early the next morning. Jon found it quite relaxing to sit on our veranda looking at the scenery, even on a cold misty day; me not so much. It was even cooler with the speed of the ship adding to the breeze. I found that if I positioned the full-length mirror on the bathroom door just right, I could sit on the bed and see what was happening outside – a much better alternative as far as I was concerned. We saw some commercial barges on the river which is mainly populated with small towns and dense forest. We also saw some nautical and lumber industries along the shore. We even saw a man burning brush, which you wouldn't see in the U.S. Jon's willingness to sit in the cold was rewarded because the sun came out about dusk and I then joined him for a beautiful sunset.

Sunset on the Svir River

Day 6 – August 15 – Kizhi Island

Kizhi Island, on Lake Onega, is only about 300 miles south of the Arctic Circle. The temperature there on this mid-August day wasn't as cold as I expected it would be considering its location. It was in the mid-60s, with the sun occasionally peeking out from behind clouds.

Kizhi Island had settlements as early as the 14th century, but they have all but disappeared with the exception of one rural settlement. In the 1960s an open-air museum was created on the island when historical wooden buildings were moved there from other parts of the region for restoration and preservation.

Kizhi is really a beautiful place with some walking trails which we unfortunately didn't have time to fully explore. Although our group wasn't the leisurely walkers group that was an option for this shore excursion, it was still a slow-moving tour. However, we did see some stunning buildings, which made up for the fact that our local tour guide was deadly dull, talking way too long in a very monotonous voice.

One of the most spectacular sites on the island is the Kizhi Pogost, a UNESCO World Heritage Site, which includes two churches and a bell tower. The Transfiguration Church, built in 1714, has 22 domes. This structure was built with a special notching technique requiring no nails. (The church was open until 1937 when Stalin closed it and the secret police executed the priest.) It includes a bell tower built in the 19th century. The Kizhi Pogost also includes the wooden Church of the Intercession, also known as the Winter Church, because yes, it was the one used in winter due to the fact that it was heated. The Kizhi Pogost is surrounded by a stone and wood wall.

We were unable to go into the Transfiguration Church, but we did enter the Winter Church where we were treated to a lovely a cappella concert by three monks. The Winter Church was filled with paintings of icons, something we saw a great deal of in churches throughout our tour. Icons are a huge part of the Russian Orthodox Church. They depict in image form religious figures or miraculous occurrences, since most people of the time were illiterate. While Russian Orthodox churches may have icons painted on the walls and ceilings, they will definitely have an iconostasis, a wooden screen on which rows of icons are painted. It separates the nave, where the congregation is located, from the altar. The altar is hidden by doors in the screen. In large churches, the screen can be quite wide and high.

22-Domed Transfiguration Church on Kizhi Island

We also saw the Church of the Resurrection of Lazarus, which was built in the 14th century and is the oldest wooden church still standing in Russia. This church was closed to visitors. As an interesting point of information, we learned that the onion dome, so common in Russia, was designed to prevent snow from accumulating on the roof.

Our tour of the island included some farmers' houses, mills, barns and granaries some of which we were able to enter and get a sense of 18th century peasant life in the region. We were able to view people doing needlework and shingle cutting. The shingle cutter we watched had actually lost parts of two fingers doing his work.

Shingle Cutter Working on Kizhi Island

Our visit to Kizhi Island lasted about 90 minutes, and we were back on the ship around 10:30 a.m. at which time we set sail for Goritzy, turning the ship southward toward our final destination of Moscow. The trip to Goritzy would be an overnight one. The staff provided us with champagne and snacks on the sun deck as we departed. Afterwards Jon went to the Sky Bar for his first of two Russian language lessons (which he found very worthwhile) while I sat on my makeshift indoor veranda reading and watching the scenery go by.

After lunch we both enjoyed a lecture given by one of the tour escorts on the Romanov Dynasty. Lake Onega was a bit rough while we were listening to the lecture, and the ship was doing a bit of rocking and rolling. Not enough to make anyone seasick, but we could definitely feel it.

Looking for something to do after the lecture, we decided to use the souvenir playing cards we bought in St. Petersburg for some games of double solitaire. We went to the table and chairs set up at one of the ends of the ship and played for a while. The table was a bit small, but we made do. One of the decks of cards contained scenes of St. Petersburg; the other had Soviet-era posters. We particularly liked that deck because the jokers were Lenin and Stalin.

Day 7 – August 16 – Goritzy

Before arriving in Goritzy, we listened to one of our tour escorts give a fascinating talk about Russian history between 1917 and 1985. He said that when he told his grandfather about going to work for an American company (Viking), his grandfather had this to say about Americans: "Jeeps, leather jackets and Spam" as he remembered the things brought to Russia by Americans during World War II.

The water on Lake Beloye was choppy, and it was colder than yesterday, but at least the sun was peeking through.

After arriving in Goritzy, we visited a local art school where we were guided by a 12-year-old student named Anastasia who spoke amazing English. She's been studying the language since the second grade. Some of the students showed us their art wares, which were for sale, and put on a short musical performance for us.

The school had photos on the wall of students who were killed in Chechnya and Afghanistan. There was also a wall of teachers who were at the school during World War II. Only one of them is still alive; she's 94.

We then drove to the Kirillo-Belozersky Monastery on the shores of Siverskoye Lake. It is located near the town of Kirillov, a village with a population of about 8,000. We were told that some of the houses in the village still don't have running water.

Founded in 1397 by St. Kirill, Kirillo-Belozersky is a complex of two monasteries having 11 churches, most dating to the 16th century. The Soviets closed the monastery in 1924, killing or imprisoning the monks and turning the complex into a museum. In 1998, monks were allowed to come back to a small portion of the monastery.

We viewed a collection of medieval icons, as well as priests' robes made with gold or silver threads and precious or semi-precious jewels. The icons are sometimes lent to other countries and are so valuable, each one requires $1.5 million worth of insurance. Among the more interesting displays was a wood carving of John the Baptist's severed head. At the end of the tour, some of the people in our group put water from the lake on their faces, because it is said to have the power to make you younger. I didn't have to do that because I'm already so youthful looking. Right?

Kirillo-Belozersky Monastery

Viking has its own dock near Kirillov which has some interesting replica buildings to view near the dock.

After returning to the *Truvor* around 5:00 p.m., Jon went to his second Russian language lesson. The "students" found it so much fun, they were sorry there weren't more than two lessons offered.

Day 8 – August 17 – Yaroslavl

Being as far north as we were, the sun was on the horizon very early. At 4:00 a.m. Jon happened to be awake and looked out our veranda. He saw a huge orange streak at the horizon to the north as the ship made its way through the Rybinsk Reservoir. This is an artificial lake formed by the Rybinsk Dam during the Stalinist era. When it was built, 150,000 people had to be resettled. The lake covers 1,768 square miles and at the time of its formation was the largest man-made body of water in the world. The reservoir sits at the northernmost point of the Volga River and is the start of the Volga-Baltic Waterway, which links the Volga to the Baltic Sea.

This morning as we sailed toward Yaroslavl, we enjoyed another fascinating presentation given by one of the tour escorts, this one about Mikhail Gorbachev and Perestroika. Neither of them was ultimately viewed very favorably by Russians. We arrived at the town's dock about 1:00 p.m. but had to wait while the ship refueled before we were able to dock. A refueling boat approached our ship while it was on the Volga River rather than refueling while tied up. So we finally docked about 3:00 and disembarked for our shore excursion.

Yaroslavl, which turned out to be a very lovely town, was founded in 1010 where the Volga River and the Kotorosl River meet. It has a picturesque park right on the shore. The park contains flowers in the shape of a bear, the symbol of the city (supposedly the city's founder Prince Yaroslavl killed a bear with his bare hands), and the number 1006, indicating the number of years since the city was founded. At the other end of the park is the Millennium of Yaroslavl Monument comprising a statue of Yaroslavl the Wise standing in front of an obelisk. In the distance you can see the Church of the Epiphany.

Park in Yaroslavl with Flowers

Nearby is the Assumption Cathedral, rebuilt starting in 2005 because the original was blown up by the Soviets in 1937. Close to the cathedral are some bells which will be installed when its belfry is built. These bells were initially going to be melted down by Stalin but were saved by sending them to Boston. They were recently returned.

In front of the cathedral is the Trinity sculpture built in 1995 to commemorate 1,000 years of Christianity in Russia. In the park behind is a World War II memorial with an eternal flame. All along the sidewalk to the cathedral there were a series of posters honoring various veterans who died in World War II. This seemed to be common throughout Russia: many monuments and memorials to those who died in the Second World War.

World War II Memorial with Assumption Cathedral in the Background

Along a path from the cathedral is a gazebo where couples stand and kiss to ensure their eternal love and togetherness. Being a romantic (or superstitious) bunch, all the couples in our group did this.

Yaroslavl was the first Christian city on the Volga, and it has the churches to prove it, so many in fact it was once known as "the city of many churches". The only other one we viewed up close was the Elijah the Prophet Church, built in the 17th century. The interior has frescoed murals depicting the life of Elijah as well as domestic life in 17th century Russia. Photos are allowed inside but only if you're willing to pay 150 rubles. In US currency, that's the equivalent of a little more than two dollars, so you may decide to spring for it. However, if you're like us, by this time you'll be getting tired of church interiors, icons and iconostases and may choose to pass. The churches are beautiful on the outside. They're all different and have gorgeous colors. But inside, we found viewing the iconography to be a bit repetitious.

There was a change of pace after this. We toured the Governor's Palace, built between 1821 and 1823 by order of Tsar Alexander I. It was the official residence for the governor of Yaroslavl between 1821 and 1917 and also served as a place for the tsar to stay when traveling in the region. The mansion currently houses some 18th, 19th and 20th century art. Our guide was a woman dressed in period dress and while acting as the governor's daughter, she led us through the house discussing its decor. She even explained how flowers and ladies' hand fans had their own languages for communicating during that time.

For me, the best part of the tour was the performance given in the ballroom by musicians and dancers. Some of the people in our group even got to participate in the dancing which included a polka and a waltz. Outside the Governor's Palace local artists put on an impressive display of lacquered boxes that were for sale. Some of the designs were incredibly ornate.

After our visit to the Governor's Palace, we were taken to Yaroslavl's indoor food market where we sampled some local cheeses provided for us by Viking. The market featured a wide variety of meats, fish, vegetables and fruit, all available in bulk (not packaged). But we ended up buying our favorite item, chocolate bars. Being a chocolate connoisseur, I can tell you Russian chocolate is quite good – not up to Belgian chocolate standards but definitely worth eating.

It was a warm, sunny day which was perfect for walking around the town center, which is how we spent our free time after the food market. We strolled in a lovely park and walked by the Alexander Nevsky Chapel, a small red brick structure built in 1892. Across the street from the chapel is a government building built during the Soviet era which still has a hammer-and-sickle carved on its exterior.

After returning to the ship and having dinner, we enjoyed a fun game of Liars Club with the other passengers in the Sky Bar. Three staff members were given an archaic English word to define. Two definitions were incorrect and one was the correct definition. Passengers playing on teams had to decide which staff member was telling the truth. Some of the definitions were so outlandish we were sure they were false, but they ended up being true. It was great fun.

All in all, the charming city of Yaroslavl proved to be one of the highlights of the entire trip. And as our local guide informed us, Yaroslavl has no earthquakes, floods, or tornadoes.

Day 9 – August 18 – Uglich

After an overnight trip down the Volga, the *Truvor* arrived in Uglich bright and early, which meant we had to be up early for our shore excursion. Our tour escort said the group would meet outside at 8:15 at the top of a 30-step staircase. She said it as if it were a dire warning – be prepared to walk up 30 steps and make sure you leave enough time to do it. Well, for anyone with any energy, it wasn't a big deal.

Uglich was founded along the banks of the Volga River supposedly in 937, although the first recorded date in which it is mentioned is 1148. The most important event that happened there occurred in 1584 when Ivan the Terrible's 8-year old son, Tsarevich Dmitry died. There are two versions of his death. In one version, the tsarevich's throat was cut by assassins sent by Boris Godunov who wanted to eliminate Dmitry's claim to the throne. The other version claims he had an epileptic seizure during a knife throwing game and fell on a knife, slitting his own throat. Believe it or not, an initial commission sided with the epilepsy theory; however a later one said it was a political murder engineered by Godunov. The church bell that was rung to announce Dmitry's death was shipped to Siberia as a form of exile (yes, the bell was exiled); it has since been returned to Uglich. A beautiful blue-domed church now stands on the site of Dmitry's death, the Church of St. Dmitry on Spilled Blood.

Church of St. Dmitry on Spilled Blood

This church is located in Uglich's kremlin. Kremlin simply means walled fort, although the wall no longer exists. To get to the kremlin, we walked over a bridge. Other buildings inside the kremlin include additional churches and the Duma (city council) building. There is also a World War II memorial. By the way, the local guide we had on this tour referred to World War II as the Great Patriotic War, which is the way they refer to it in Russia. Of course our trip back to the ship wouldn't be complete without walking by vendors who had lots and lots of souvenirs for sale.

The next portion of our Uglich tour included a visit to the home of an Uglich resident. Vladimir lives with his wife and daughter in a small house with an extensive backyard garden that has fruits and vegetables. He has a modest home with linoleum floors and lots of books. He said a one-bedroom house goes for $30,000 in Uglich and $300,000 in Moscow. We were invited to take part in a brief lunch in his dining room with brown bread, pickles, apple cake and his own homemade vodka. We drank several toasts as he told us about his life in Uglich. Vladimir and his wife are jewelers who do fine silver work which is enameled elsewhere in a local factory. Among his crafts was a stunning spoon he made that has a stained glass effect when held up to light. I would have purchased it if he had offered it for sale. Some of his company's more expensive offerings can go for as much as $25, 000. Vladimir said he thinks Putin is a good leader; this was a common theme among Russians we spoke to. Then our group visited his large (by Chicago standards) backyard garden in which he grew potatoes, pears, apples and grapes. Also gracing his backyard garden was a newly constructed chicken coop.

Our stop with Vladimir was the end of our tour in Uglich. The ship left for Moscow at 11:45 a.m. One of our Russian tour escorts gave a lecture in the afternoon on the ship, this one about Medvedev and Putin. Afterwards, since it was such a lovely warm day (in the 70s), we spent time sitting on the veranda (yes, both of us!). There were lots of fishermen on the Volga, in boats and along the shore. Not only were the fishermen shirtless, but a number of them were in Speedos. Having observed so many of them on this day, we can only say that Putin riding a horse with his shirt off may be normal Russian behavior. At least Putin hasn't gone so far as to wear Speedos!

Day 10 – August 19 – Moscow

Jon woke up three times during the night (what can I say – he's old) and looked out our veranda each time to see what he could see; and wouldn't you know it, each time the ship was going through a lock. Well, we were told there are lots of locks on the way to Moscow. Timing is everything.

Our cruise toward Moscow took us on the Moscow Canal from the Volga until we reached the Moscow River. Again we saw a lot of fishermen, as well as hikers, and even heard a rooster crowing. While sailing we had a Q&A with our three Russian tour guides who answered questions about modern day Russia. Among the interesting things we learned were that home loans cost about 12% and that, though there are both private and public health care in Russia, the public care is very slow. Or as one of our tour escorts put it, "If you're going to see a doctor, you should be healthy before you go."

We docked in Moscow about 1:00 p.m. As in St. Petersburg, we had to dock well out of town, at the North River Terminal. The main terminal building was probably once quite impressive but it has become quite rundown.

The weather during our three days in Moscow was quite warm, in the 80s, as Moscow is further south than any of our previous stops. It varied between sunny and rainy, often in the same day.

We had a tour of the city this afternoon and again as in St. Petersburg, we chose the longer, more intensive walking tour rather than the bus tour. To get to the city center from the dock we had about a 20 minute walk through a nearby park and a pedestrian underpass to the metro station. The metro train we rode was an older one, similar to the one in St. Petersburg in that it was not air conditioned; it did however offer exceptionally quick acceleration. Be careful of the rapidly closing doors. Jon likened their operation to a guillotine. Our local guide took us to several different metro stations. We thought we had to change trains to get downtown, but her purpose was to show us the different stations which have fascinating architecture and designs. The art in the stations includes mosaics, statues and stained glass. One station we went to, the Mayakovskaya Station, has marble walls and beautiful mosaics in the ceiling. The Ploschad Revolyutsii (Revolution Square) Station has 76 statues of people of the Soviet Union, such as farmers, athletes, industrial workers and soldiers. One of the statues of a soldier with a dog is said to bring good luck if you rub the dog's nose, so of course we all did. The dog's nose is shiny from all the rubbing. Another statue showed a rather grim looking soldier holding a handgun, which seems somewhat strange in this day and age. Some of the metro stations are very far down underground. For instance, the Mayakovskaya Station is 100 feet down.

Ceiling Mosaic in Mayakovskaya Metro Station

Our stop after the metro tour was Red Square, which was extremely crowded with tourists. When we were there, they were preparing for some sort of military celebration, and bleachers were being installed on the square. As a result, we couldn't actually walk on the square; we could only walk around it. Unfortunately we weren't able to take in the whole expanse of the square from one end to the other. There went my vision of having my picture taken on Red Square with St. Basil's Cathedral in the background. We did still get to see the church which many consider Moscow's most famous building.

St. Basil's Cathedral in Red Square

GUM (pronounced goom) Department Store is right by Red Square. It's a huge building, taking up most of the east side of the square. The building has three floors with a striking wooden escalator and overhead walkways. There is a central courtyard with a fountain in the center that is covered with a glass roof. When we were there, the fountain was filled with watermelons. The building houses lots of upscale boutiques and retail chains. But before you can see any of this, you'll have to go through a metal detector at the entrance.

Our local guide recommended we try the ice cream that was being sold on the first floor. She said it was just like the ice cream she had as a child during the Soviet era. I can't comment on that, but it was delicious, as rich and creamy as some of the gelato we had in Italy.

Just before entering the building, our guide pointed out the restrooms which were down a flight of stairs. We were both a bit startled at first in our respective bathrooms, because the first few stalls contained eastern toilets, basically just holes in the floor with foot rests on either side. If you go there, don't despair. Walk a little further back into the bathroom and you'll see the western toilets. It's nice to know they're willing to accommodate everyone.

Fountain Filled with Watermelons at GUM

We had some free time so we walked by Lenin's Tomb and viewed the wares of the multitude of vendors. The vendors had more of the same souvenirs that we had seen up to this point, but there were a lot more of them.

Just outside Red Square is Moscow's Tomb of the Unknown Soldier, dedicated to the Soviet soldiers killed during World War II. It's located in a park right outside the Kremlin wall. It has an eternal flame with a guard on either side. We were lucky enough to get there just as the changing of the guard was occurring. Immediately outside the Kremlin walls is a large statue of General Zhukov, a hero of the Second World War.

Tomb of the Unknown Soldier in Moscow

After meeting up again with the other passengers in our group, our guide led us on a walk to the Cathedral of Christ the Savior. This is a relatively new church, built between 1995 and 2000. It stands on the site of the original 19th century church that was destroyed in 1931 on Stalin's orders. Stalin had planned to use this location for a Palace of Soviets, with a 300-plus foot statue of Lenin at the top. Construction was started in 1937 but halted during World War II. It was never restarted, and during the 1950s, the world's largest open-air swimming pool was built there. In 1995, the Russian Orthodox Church got permission from the government to rebuild the church.

The current church is the tallest Orthodox Christian church in the world, having an overall height of 338 feet. We found it to be dark inside and we noticed the absence of pews. That must be how they can get 10,000 worshippers inside. It is filled with painted iconic frescoes, and we were struck by the beauty of a carved manger scene on display there.

The cathedral observes strict dress codes for its visitors. We saw one man become quite upset when he was denied entry because he was wearing shorts; however a woman in shorts was allowed in, which we were told was also forbidden. Women are asked to cover their heads with a hat, scarf, jacket hood, etc. and men are asked to remove their hats.

Afterward, we walked over the Great Stone Bridge for excellent distant views of the cathedral and of the Kremlin wall. The Kremlin towers still feature five-point red stars which are illuminated and rotate with the wind. The stars are made of ruby glass. The towers were constructed in the 15th century. They were originally topped with the two-headed eagle which was Russia's coat of arms at that time. In the mid-1930s the Soviet government ordered the eagles be replaced with the stars that still top them today. Gorky Park was also visible during our rainy, yet quite lovely walk along this impressive bridge. From this bridge you can also see a building called "Stalin's Birthday Cake," a 1930s-era skyscraper which bristles with lots of Stalinist spires.

View of the Kremlin from Across the Moscow River

We also saw a 320-plus foot high monument to Peter the Great sitting on an island in the Moscow River. It was created in 1997 to honor 300 years of the Russian navy, which was established by the tsar. There has been a lot of controversy surrounding the statue. Many people consider it to be one of the ugliest things they've ever seen, and some question why Moscow should have a statue of a man who intensely disliked the city and preferred to live in St. Petersburg. There's a story that the design of the statue was to be of Christopher Columbus to celebrate the 500th anniversary of his 1492 voyage; however when no city wanted to buy it, the design was repurposed. Whatever is true, we'll let you decide what you think of it here.

Monument to Peter the Great in the Moscow River

And as it is disposed to do when we're on a walking tour, it was raining. Still the city of Moscow looked very pretty along the river with the Kremlin within our view.

That evening we sat on the bus and ate a quick boxed dinner, which had been given to us upon leaving the ship. We had to eat quickly because there wasn't enough time for a leisurely dinner before attending that evening's performance of the Russian Folk Orchestra. On the way to the concert hall, we had a few minutes to walk on the Luzhkov Bridge and see the iron trees with locks placed by newlyweds. Instead of placing the locks on bridges as has been done in other cities, they place them on these trees.

Trees with Locks on the Luzhkov Bridge

We weren't particularly looking forward to this evening since it was at the end of a busy day. How wrong we were! It was so much fun! The Russian Folk Orchestra is a group of young musicians each of whom is a national champion in their chosen instrument. They performed in a small, intimate theater which allowed us to view their playing up close. The instruments they played included balalaikas, guslis (a multi-string plucked instrument), domras (a Russian string instrument with a long neck and round body) and xylophones. Several of the orchestra members played solos which gave us a chance to see how beautifully they played their instruments, and there was also a singer who accompanied them on a few songs. They played popular songs such as Lara's Theme from Dr. Zhivago, as well as lesser known (to us) Russian folk songs. They also asked for two volunteers from the audience to "assist" them in playing a couple of the instruments. That was quite a fun bit of audience participation.

Day 11 – August 20 – Moscow

Since we didn't choose either of this morning's optional tours – one to the monastery at Sergiev Posad and the other to the Tretyakov Gallery – we were free until 3:00. We decided to take a walk in the park seen during the previous day on the way to the metro station. We ended up back near the metro station where there were some modern shops and a very interesting, well-stocked grocery store with live fish and lots of fresh fruits, vegetables, meats, breads, cheeses and nuts. As in the farmer's market in Yaroslavl, there seemed to be much more bulk produce and much less packaged food than you would see in an American supermarket. There were a number of statues in the park on the walk over to the stores with inscriptions in Russian that we were completely unable to decipher.

At 3:00 we did a two-hour optional tour to the Cosmonaut Museum. Since it was a Saturday, traffic wasn't too heavy and it only took about an hour to get there. The official name of the museum is Memorial Museum of Cosmonautics, and it was fascinating. The museum is visible from quite a distance due to the enormous rocket sculpture that sits atop the museum. Built in 1981 but reconstructed in 2009, it focuses mostly on the Soviet space program and has approximately 85,000 different items, featuring everything from Sputnik, the first artificial Earth satellite, to the International Space Station, including life-size models of capsules, rockets, and moon landing craft. There is also a full-scale model of a MIR space station module, which we were able to walk through, allowing us to view the bathroom facilities up close (I thought I'd mention that because people are generally curious about those arrangements in space). The museum also has a couple of donations from the United States – the space suit worn by Michael Collins on Apollo 11 and some moon rocks. Everything in the museum is written is Russian, so it was good to have a local guide with us to explain what we were viewing. If you want to take photographs inside, it will cost you 230 rubles (about $3.50).

The museum has what might be called some bizarre displays as well. For instance, there's a life-size diorama of the cosmonauts who ended up landing a capsule with mechanical problems off course in a snowy forest in Siberia. They were sweating profusely inside their suits and were at risk for hypothermia. Because of the trees, their rescue had to take place on skis. Another exhibit features Belka and Strelka, two dogs, now stuffed, who were sent into space for a day and returned safely, the first living beings from Earth to do so. Belka eventually had six puppies with a male dog named Pushok. One of the pups named Pushinka was given as a gift to President John Kennedy and his family by Nikita Khrushchev in 1961. Pushinka's descendants are still alive today.

Belka and Strelka

They always say to exit through the gift shop, but this museum's shop was uninspiring. It was small with a few tee shirts and pads of note paper and only one pamphlet in English. There were some books, but they were in Russian. If you go to the gift shop, don't expect much. Also, the clerk in the gift shop refused to change a

1,000 ruble note (about 15 dollars) for a customer; apparently she didn't have sufficient change.

The museum is actually located in the base of a 350 foot tall monument known as the Monument to the Conquerors of Space. It's a sculpture of a rocket rising on its exhaust plume. To us the rocket on top of the monument looked like something you'd see in the old Buck Rogers TV show. On the sides are relief sculptures that depict people involved in the space program such as scientists and engineers. Of course it also includes Lenin. I say of course because we saw statues of Lenin in just about every town we visited. Given how egotistical Putin is, I'm surprised he hasn't replaced them all.

Monument to the Conquerors of Space

In front of the monument is a statue of Konstantin Tsiolkovsky, a Soviet rocket scientist and one of the pioneers of astronautics. To the south of the monument is the Cosmonauts Alley, with busts of Soviet cosmonauts, as well as a statue of Sergei Korolev, the founder of Russian astronautics who designed many of Russia's first rockets

When traveling in Moscow always be alert for Soviet era statues. They're everywhere and some are utterly amazing. We missed one, a statue of a Soviet era man which must have been 20 feet high, because we sat on the wrong side of the bus on the way back.

Day 12 – August 21 – Moscow

Today, our last day in Moscow, we took another optional tour, this one to the Kremlin Armory which contains tsarist artifacts, jewelry and armor. If this were a weekday, it would take about an hour to get there from the ship, but since it was Sunday, it only took about 30 minutes.

For me, this was the highlight of our trip. Unfortunately, photographs are not allowed inside the Armory, so I can't show you just how amazing it is. Hopefully my description will convey it. The Armory contains dresses, robes and crowns worn by royalty such as Catherine the Great and Peter the Great. Catherine's coronation gown has an 18 inch waist. Of course, she was only 16 at the time she wore it, and based on paintings of her as an older woman, her waist got significantly larger as she aged.

The museum also houses a number of ornate royal carriages, some with wheels so large they could never be used. Some of the carriages required the driver to sit in back because no one was allowed to have their back to the tsar. There were also two royal sleighs, probably not found in too many other countries. And there were two tiny carriages for the children.

The Armory houses a variety of other items including weaponry; armor; religious vestments; gold and silver tableware; jeweled and fur-lined crowns; and thrones. One of my favorites was the dual throne for 10- year-old Peter (who eventually became Peter the Great) and his 15-year-old brother Ivan who were crowned together. A double throne was built for them with a secret hiding place in the back for their advisors to whisper to them.

The most famous items in the Armory are the Faberge eggs. The Faberge firm was founded in St. Petersburg in 1842 by Gustav Faberge. The company became world-famous under Gustav's son Carl. Carl was asked to make a jeweled egg for Tsar Alexander III to present to his wife at Easter. It was such a success, that the giving of a Faberge Easter egg became an annual tradition among the Romanovs. Each egg has a surprise inside. One of the eggs has paintings of Tsar Nicholas II's children. Each portrait is in a diamond frame. Another egg contains a pure gold model of a train that was the first to run along the Trans-Siberian Railway. Each car is about the size of one of your fingers. The train actually folds up to fit inside the egg! These are just two of the 10 amazing eggs in the armory.

Just as an fyi, the late media mogul Malcom Forbes had a collection of nine Faberge eggs that he displayed in New York. A Russian tycoon bought the entire collection when Forbes' estate planned to auction it off. The eggs are now displayed in a museum in St. Petersburg. Of the 50 Faberge eggs that were created, 19 are now in Russia. The whereabouts of eight are unknown.

There's a separate museum located in the Armory called the Diamond Fund. It's not part of the Kremlin museums, and it has its own rules. We didn't get to see it, but from what I understand, it's pretty spectacular, so if you're there and you can arrange it, I think it might be worth your while. The Diamond Fund houses Russia's crown jewels. Among the items is the Great Imperial Crown, first worn by Catherine the Great, covered with 4,936 diamonds. There is also the Imperial Scepter with a 190-carat diamond known as the Orlov Diamond, named for the count who purchased it for Catherine the Great. If that's not enough to make you want to go, nothing will.

Now back to our day. After the Armory, our tour continued in the Kremlin. We walked by the office building once used by Lenin and Stalin and currently used by Putin. It's technically the official residence of Russia's president, but Putin uses it just as his office. We also viewed the Great Kremlin Palace, a beautiful green and white building that used to be the Moscow residence of the tsars and today is used for official receptions.

Official Residence of Russia's President in the Kremlin

There is a huge bronze canon in the Kremlin, called the Tsar Canon that was made in 1586. It's more than 16 feet long and weighs more than 39 tons. It has never been used and now stands on one of the squares in the Kremlin.

There is also a Tsar Bell that is the largest bell in the world. It weighs over 200 tons and stands over 20 feet high and 21-1/2 feet across. There was a fire in Moscow in 1737 that spread to the Kremlin while the bell was still in its molding pit. When the flames were being put out, cold water fell on the bell. The difference between the hot and cold temperatures caused a portion of the bell to crack and fall off. The bell can now be seen on a stone pedestal with the 11-ton broken chunk next to it.

Of course our tour of the Kremlin wouldn't be complete without seeing more churches. I remember thinking it was good we were heading home the next day, because I had my fill of churches and icons. The Kremlin even has a square called Cathedral Square with cathedrals on it. Dormition Cathedral, or Church of the Assumption, is the main cathedral. It's the cathedral where all the tsars were crowned. This is the only one of the churches we visited inside, and its interior is covered with 17th century frescoes and icons.

One interesting anomaly inside the Kremlin was an out-of-place looking government building constructed during the Khrushchev era. The building is the State Kremlin Palace and was used for Communist Party meetings. It is now used as a concert hall. Though modern and impressive, the building really doesn't fit with the famous historical buildings inside the Kremlin. Our guide told us that since the Moscow Kremlin is a UNESCO site, the building could not be removed, though if you see it, it's obvious that it doesn't belong there.

After having lunch back on the ship, we joined our last tour, another optional one, to the Jewish Museum and Tolerance Center. Built in 2012, it's located in a former bus garage that has been restored to the tune of $50 million. It is supposedly the world's largest Jewish museum. As you might guess from its construction date, it is very modern and very high-tech. Before touring the museum, we viewed a 4-D movie covering Judaism from Genesis to the destruction of the second Temple by the Romans in 70 C.E. We wore 3-D glasses, but it was billed as 4-D because we were sprayed lightly with water during Noah's flood and our seats rocked back and forth during the scenes of destruction.

This modern museum has multimedia, interactive exhibits about the Jewish experience in Russia from the 19th century to the present. There's a multimedia exhibit covering the Jewish Diaspora, showing the location of Jews throughout the world, as well as photographs of them in those locations. I was surprised when I viewed a photo of Jews in China; it was obvious from the picture that they had intermarried with the local people, something I had thought they were reluctant to do in the past. There's a large exhibit covering life in the shtetl. Press a button and a hologram shows a family celebrating the Sabbath, or sit with worshippers in a synagogue and press a button to read from a digital Torah. There are exhibits covering pogroms, World War II and the Holocaust, discrimination during the Soviet years, as well as the current resurgence of Judaism in Russia.

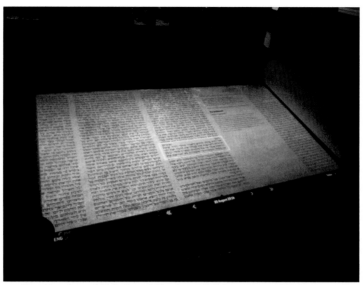

Interactive Torah and Pointer at the Jewish Museum and Tolerance Center

One of the museum's fascinating high-tech features was a series of tables that served as interactive screens to view short, two-minute movies on various historical topics. We were viewing a couple of very intriguing videos on pogroms when a museum staffer told us, politely, not to lean on the tables as they were "fragile." So I guess there is some more work to be done on those particular devices, though the videos alone were worth a visit to the museum.

It's an amazing museum, but it could be improved in a couple of ways. First, only about half of the exhibits had English translations. Second, there were too many different videos loudly playing in too small an area. It was sometimes difficult to hear our guide. Also, for those who wanted to buy a book in the gift shop about the museum or its subject matter (yes, like us), there were no books in English, save a large, heavy $75 volume. Several of our fellow visitors had the same problem; I don't know if they bought the weighty volume or not.

After the museum, we headed back to the ship. Because of an incident that occurred with our bus driver on this day, I'll take the opportunity to tell you about Russian drivers. Many of them leave something to be desired. Traveling on Moscow's Ring Road on the way back to the boat, we often faced very heavy traffic. Also, readily apparent were a number of fender-bender accidents. The most unusual traffic sight though was a woman in a VW Beetle, who had apparently been in an accident and had taped the exploded airbag back to the steering wheel in her car.

When we got back to the dock after visiting the Jewish Museum, two buses were turning left out of the road our bus was turning right into. They saw our bus coming and didn't stop. Nor did they back up. There was a nice Mexican standoff for a while with one of the outgoing bus drivers getting quite upset and gesticulating wildly. It was nice to see our driver Victor remain very calm, and he won. The other buses backed up, which was something to see since there was a whole line of cars behind them at this point. There was also one idiot in a Volvo who tried to pass everyone on the shoulder, but he was forced to retreat. It's amazing to observe the indifference Muscovites show to a huge object (the bus) bearing down on them on a narrow road and not moving until absolutely necessary.

Day 13 – August 22 – Chicago

We flew home to Chicago via Munich, but first we had to get out of Moscow. We learned from the ship staff that there are three airports in Moscow. Unfortunately the Viking staff in the home office booked us out of Domodedovo, the one that's farthest away. And by farthest away, I mean two hours away. I think the airport you end up at depends on which airline you're flying. We were flying Lufthansa, also unfortunately. I haven't liked Lufthansa since the time I was flying in economy and they showed us a video of all the perks the people were getting in business class.

Anyway, back to the airport being two hours away. That meant we had to get up at 4:00 a.m. to catch a 9:00 a.m. flight. Viking was very accommodating and opened up the Panorama Bar for all the early departing guests so we could have breakfast.

When we got to the airport, we had to go through an x-ray before we could even enter the building. Given the state of the world today, I think other airports could learn from this. One of our Russian tour escorts accompanied us to the airport and made sure we, and our luggage, got to our correct airline. After saying good-bye, we checked in at the Lufthansa counter, went through passport control and then security. Every airport is different in terms of security. At this one, we didn't have to take our shoes off or remove our electronic items from our carry-on bags, but Jon had to remove his cloth belt and his watch which had a leather (not metal) band.

We walked by a bookstore in the terminal which was closed. Of course it was closed; it was only 6 o'clock in the morning. There was a sign on the door that said in English, "Technical Timeout".

The long wait for our flight was alleviated somewhat by watching the passengers around us. Behind us sat a group of Germans talking animatedly, occasionally in English, about cars. More interesting still was a group of high school musicians, heading for some sort of event in Munich. The boys opposite us opened their bag to reveal two sandwiches from KFC (which they promptly ate) as well as an entire loaf of rye bread and a tray of some sort of lunch meat. We wondered whether they could take that on the plane, but after watching them eat the sandwiches, we were both pretty sure there wouldn't be much left by the time they boarded.

Is a Russian River Cruise for You?

Russia has a lot to offer tourists. There's so much to see and learn about. You'll come home with fabulous memories and a wealth of knowledge. For those of you of a certain age, Russia, or the Soviet Union as it was formerly known, was a great unknown world power and adversary. Times have changed (somewhat) and the opportunity to visit all those places you heard about for years makes Russia well worth visiting.

Whether river cruising is the right way for you to see the country can depend on certain factors:

Not having to pack and unpack your luggage every time you move to a new location is a definite plus. You unpack once and that's it for 13 days. The ship is your hotel. If you've ever taken a bus tour where you change hotels every one or two days, you know what a chore it is to have to pack up in the morning when you're leaving. It's a real treat to be able to unpack once for the whole trip.

I think you have to have the right disposition for river cruising in Russia. You can enjoy it for a while if the temperature is warm enough to sit on your veranda, the sun isn't shining in your eyes while you're doing so, and there's something to see on the river. I've never taken a river cruise on the Rhine, but I imagine it's a bit different, with castles and picturesque towns clustered close together. In Russia, the towns are far apart during the days you're cruising between St. Petersburg and Moscow. Also if after a while you want to get up and do something – walk somewhere – be active – then river cruising in Russia may not be for you. The five days we spent between St. Petersburg and Moscow included only one stop each day and, compared to the time on the ship, it was short. The ship is small; there is no fitness center and there's little room to walk around the decks. If you have any kind of energy to expend, this cruise may not be for you. I don't mean to imply that the trip wasn't fun; it was. I'm just not sure about the mode of transportation.

A number of the passengers on our cruise appeared to be older than us. They walked more slowly than we like to walk. Some of them had canes and one even needed a wheel chair. The tour escorts walked quite slowly as well. Even when there was an optional "leisure tour" for those people, the guides on our tours walked more slowly than we would have liked. I'm not saying I want a marathon pace, just a little quicker. If you're the same, you may want to think twice about a Russian River cruise.

If you decide to take a river cruise, should you do so with Viking? Well, of course that's up to you. There are several river cruise companies out there. When planning the trip, our travel agent and I had some problems with Viking's customer service concerning the included flights. I could write a chapter on those issues alone. To make it worse, they acted as if they didn't care. However, once we were on the cruise, I forgot about all that. We found the accommodations and staff to be excellent.

We strongly encourage you to visit Russia, whichever type of tour you choose. From its fascinating history to its incredible architecture, it definitely deserves a look.

Appendix - Vladimir Putin: New Russian Tsar or Tee Shirt Hero?

When we first visited St. Petersburg in 2009, we were both impressed not only by the beauty of the Church of Our Savior on the Spilled Blood, but also by the large number of souvenir vendors in the plaza outside the church. You could get everything there - Russian lacquered boxes, nesting dolls of all descriptions (including those of US sports teams) and every sort of knick-knack. What we didn't see a lot of at that time were Putin souvenirs - just a few Putin nesting dolls as part of a Russian leader series.

Oh how things have changed since then. Now, there are Putin refrigerator magnets, tee shirts, mugs (see photo on Day 3 above) and just about every souvenir you can imagine with Putin's face on it.

Of course in 2009 Vladimir Putin was only Russia's Prime Minister, not its President, as he has been since 2012. Though arguably he has been the sole power in Russia since he first became acting President in 1999, clearly his stock in Russia has soared, and that became very evident with every day we spent in Russia on our river cruise. Whether it was photos of Putin painting a matryoshka doll in a storefront in Mandrogy, or our guide at Catherine's Palace pointing out a photo of Putin entertaining world leaders (while at the same time ignoring a photo of Gorbachev), references to the Russian leader seemed to be everywhere.

Looking at the various souvenirs we wondered whether they were meant to portray Putin as a Russian hero or whether they were meant to be a joke for tourists. Or were they meant to be a lesson for tourists? For example, the tee shirt below clearly shows Putin as a strong, powerful leader, yet the inscription is in English.

Putin as Military Hero on a Tee Shirt

Or how about the tee-shirt we saw in Uglich: a stern Putin as schoolmaster seeming to discipline tiny school children with the faces of Angela Merkel, Francoise Hollande and Barack Obama. We asked one of our excellent tour escorts what the inscription in Russian said. He translated it as "Do you understand what you did?" What the Western leaders did was adopt sanctions against Russia, which our guides pointed out were very, very unpopular there.

More than once during our travels, our Viking tour escorts and our local guides made mention of the fact that the European Union's sanctions against Russia had not worked. In fact, they said the sanctions had made Russia stronger. No longer would Russia need to import foreign food, since local farmers could now grow much of what was missing. This was pointed out with much pride in the local products. To Russians the sanctions were an attack on Russia, and Putin's standing up to the sanctions (as noted on the tee shirt) made him that much more popular with the Russian people.

On one of the last days of the tour when our tour escorts submitted to a question and answer session from the audience, Jon asked them simply why Putin was so popular in Russia. One of the escorts said *sotto voce*, "Because you keep asking about him." Another escort pointed out how Putin had stood up to the oligarchs and run-away capitalists. In particular he mentioned one event in which a wealthy business owner was threatening to close a factory, the sole employer in a Russian town. Putin intervened and ordered the owner to keep the factory open. According to our escort, Putin saved the day.

The Russians we met seemed to view Putin with affection. He was standing up for the common people against the oligarchs and those in the West who don't respect Russia. And for a while we started to somewhat appreciate their point of view. Then we arrived in Munich on the way back home and we saw this headline in the *International Herald Tribune* which quickly brought us back to reality:

MORE OF THE KREMLIN'S OPPONENTS ARE ENDING UP DEAD

On August 22 we were in the Domodedovo Airport in Moscow waiting for our flight to Munich. Jon still didn't have a Putin souvenir, which he confessed he wanted rather badly, so he wandered about looking for souvenir stands. And sure enough he found one in the vast airport complex. After some searching, he succumbed and bought a refrigerator magnet with Putin eying us narrowly through a pair of dark sunglasses. Perfect.

It's on our refrigerator here in Chicago now. We think the other magnets are afraid of it.

About The Authors

Marcy and Jon Ruesch live in Chicago. They love to travel, both nationally and internationally. In addition to travel, they enjoy movies, theater, and bike riding along Chicago's lakefront. Although they only recently returned from their Russian river cruise, they're already thinking about where they want to travel to next. Stay tuned for their next book to find out where they go!

Other Books by Marcy and Jon Ruesch

If you enjoyed this book, you may also enjoy

Touring Italy on a Gelato a Day: Travel Highlights, Mishaps and Adventures, an account of our experiences in Venice, Lake Como, Cinque Terre, Florence, San Gimignano, Assisi, Rome, and Ostia Antica.

The Highs and Lows of Austria, Germany and Switzerland: Travel Adventures in Mountains, Meadows and Towns, an account of our experiences in Vienna, Halstatt and Salzburg, Austria; Bratislava, Slovakia; the Alps and the Lauterbrunnen Valley, Switzerland; and Munich, Nurenberg, Lindau, the Rhine and Mosel River Valleys, Germany.

Planning for Europe: What To Know Before You Go, an essential book for those traveling to Europe for the first time. It answers the questions you have as well as some you haven't thought of.

Traveling Through History: Civil War Sites In Natchez and Vicksburg, Mississippi, a description of our excursions as we explored this country's Civil War-era history in some amazing locations.

Ready for Take-Off: Travel Journal, a great way to preserve travel memories.

Made in the USA
Middletown, DE
12 May 2018